Take Charge of Your IRA:

Avoid Tax Traps and Family Squabbles

by
Richard W. Duff, JD, CLU
and
Steven M. Broughton

Steven is an Investment Advisor Representative with
Legacy Advisory Services, an SEC registered investment advisor.

Take Charge of Your IRA:
Avoid Tax Traps and Family Squabbles

Published by RWD Enterprises,
4401 So. Quebec St., G 100
Denver, CO 80237 U.S.A.
tel 303-756-3599
fax 303-691-0474
RWDuffCLU@aol.com
www.RWDuff.com

Book and cover design by Robert Marcus Graphics, Sebastopol, California.
Cartoons by Alex Kosakowski, Chicago, IL.
Printed in the United States of America.
First Edition, 2003.

ISBN 1-882703-02-2

To the reader: Know that Richard Duff is the sole author of this book except for Mr. Broughton's portion and Mr. Broughton is not receiving any royalty or commission from sales thereof. Neither Mr. Duff nor Mr. Broughton are engaged in giving tax or legal advice. Before making any changes in your financial planning based on ideas contained in this book, you should consult an attorney, CPA or other tax advisor.

Acknowledgments

To Victoria and Holly, my pride and inspiration. I love you both!

A Word From Steve Broughton

Over my seventeen-year career it never ceases to amaze me how little importance most people put on one of their largest assets! In a properly managed 401k or IRA the goal is to have it grow to help provide for your financial security. "Take Charge of Your IRA", outlines how to manage your account and avoid costly tax traps and family squabbles.

One of the most important things to realize right from the start is just how important an asset this is for your retirement. Many companies today are reducing or eliminating defined benefit and pension plans that provide a lifetime payout at retirement. Even more disconcerting is that most of these pension plans are NOT guaranteed by the company! If the company files for bankruptcy, merges or is bought out by another company, your payments can be significantly reduced or stopped completely. However, defined benefit plans and 401k plans are usually protected within a trust.

It's time to "Take Charge of Your IRA"! The first question to ask yourself is, "Do I want to manage this myself or should I work with an investment advisor?". While many people can invest themselves, it is my recommendation that you should work with an investment professional. Why? Because a professional money manager has an objective point of view. All of us are very subjective when it comes to OUR money! Becoming emotional while investing is one the biggest mistakes anyone can make and can lead to bad decisions with negative results. Finding an investment professional that you can develop a relationship is an important key. Remember though, that at the end of the day this is your account. Make sure you are involved in the investment decisions and track the performance of your account.

It is also important to know your risk tolerance. Risk tolerance is the process of understanding how much risk you are willing to take in the hopes of achieving the returns you want to have. Many people take moderate to high-risk positions are not aware that they are doing so until their account drops 25-50%. It is crucial to understand what risk you are willing to take and make sure that your investment actually has that amount of risk in the portfolio. Several years ago, a client of mine decided to put the bulk of his IRA with a friend of his he had recently seen at a school reunion. This friend had become an investment guru in the mid west. Knowing the client and his wife, I knew them to be people with little to no tolerance for risk. I cautioned them about putting money in this investment because it went against their objectives. A year later at a review in the office, (I'm sure he had forgotten the conversation we had) he complained at how much stress the investment had caused he and his wife. He stated how that had interfered with their marriage and he never should have made that investment. The interesting thing to me was that the investment had not made much money, but really hadn't lost any either. It was just the uncertainty of the risk went against their nature. It is so important for each person to understand what risk he or she is willing to take regardless of the potential returns.

It is also critical that you understand the tax consequences of your IRA. While the federal government has authorized special tax incentives when the money goes in, there are also tax consequences when you withdraw money from your IRA. It is important to understand what those ramifications are and use them to your best interest. For example, I have many clients who call me around Christmas wanting to receive a check from their IRA for the holidays. What I tell them is that if they make the withdrawal before January first, they will pay taxes in the current year. If they can use other liquid funds for the time being and take the money out after January 1st, they can delay the taxes until the following year. Depending on the income for that year the client may want to do one or the other. It is just important to understand what the tax consequences are when liquidating funds from the IRA.

One of the most important functions I perform as an Investment Advisor Representative is to educate my clients and work with them so that together, we can assess how much risk they're willing to tolerate to reach their financial goals. I have over 17 years of experience working with people, just like you, to help them reach their goals and objectives. Income needs, marital status, children, risk tolerance and tax issues affect how an IRA should be managed. The more you know, the better decisions you may be able to make regarding your account. In the ensuing chapters, this book will discuss many things; contribution limits, tax status, withdrawing funds, etc. But remember, your IRA can be one of the largest assets you have at retirement. I suggest you work with an IRA specialist and "Take Charge of Your IRA!".

Introduction

Individual Retirement Accounts (IRAs) are truly special. Where else can you get an IRS approved tax shelter that you control? These actually come in two basic types - a *traditional* IRA where there is a tax deduction up front and everything taken is taxable later, or a *Roth* where your contributions aren't deductible but distributions can be tax-free. The *bottom line:* As long as your money stays in these plans, you don't pay taxes on the profit. You can have either, or both, as long as what you pay in doesn't exceed limits in the law.

It's not so much the type of IRA (traditional or Roth) that counts - or the investment choices that you manage. They aren't difficult. The tricky part is how you and your beneficiaries eventually receive distributions from the IRA. You will want to take income when needed; while trying to leave tax-sheltered money in the account as long as possible. How you balance these objectives without paying high income and penalty taxes is the secret to good IRA management. This is what *Take Charge of Your IRA* is all about.

After you read this book, you'll surely feel empowered to discuss matters with lawyers, accountants, and financial planners. Perhaps, you'll want to have an "IRA meeting" with them - a lunch where you buy and everyone makes a few suggestions. It's your capital, and you should take advantage of everything permitted by the system, before the system takes complete advantage of you. After all, the only thing certain about having money is that someone else always wants it too.

This material can be dry so I've made every effort to keep your attention. Each "chapter" covers a specific situation common to many IRA owners. I've even included cartoons and some funny quotes to kick it up a notch. If you have questions after you read this, have your key advisers contact me at 303-756-3599 (fax 303-691-0474), (e-mail RWDuffCLU@aol.com) for clarification on any of these points. I really want you to get something out of this book.

Here's a sampling of what's ahead. You'll learn:

- How much you can contribute to an IRA in the years ahead (chapter 1);
- When it is right to convert a traditional IRA to a Roth (chapter 2);
- The special qualities of a gifted Roth (chapter 3);
- The unique advantages of IRA rollovers (chapters 4 and 8);
- About the 6 percent, 10 percent and 50 percent IRA penalty taxes (chapters 1, 5 and 6);

- What lies ahead once you inherit an IRA (chapter 13);
- Whether to cash-out, take minimum distributions, or annuitize the account at retirement (chapters 6 and 12);
- The differences between IRA individual beneficiaries and trusts for their benefit (chapters 7, 8, 9 and 17);
- Whether you should leave an account directly to your spouse (chapters 8 and 9);
- Why all the emphasis on stretch-like IRAs (chapter 10);
- How to resolve IRA problems in second marriages (chapter 11);
- When accounts are part of a large estate (chapter 17);
- What to expect from an IRA custodian (chapter 10);
- When it is best to leave an IRA to charity (chapter 16);

and much, much more.

In short, this is a general primer that details imaginative solutions to problems most IRA owners have. Since laws vary from state to state, always discuss your IRA issues with qualified attorneys, CPAs, financial planners and other professionals. Give them a copy of this book and ask for help. Believe me, they'll have plenty of ideas that apply to your facts and circumstances.

Best wishes.

Richard W. Duff

Take Charge of Your IRA:
Avoid Tax Traps and Family Squabbles

Table of Contents

1.

Going on three decades: IRAs have come a long way!

"Frugality includes all other virtues." Cicero

On September 2, 1974, Congress passed the Employee Retirement Income Security Act (ERISA). Without a doubt, this was the most comprehensive overhaul of the U.S. private pension system in history. It also included the first rules for Individual Retirement Accounts (IRAs).

IRAs were introduced in the mid-70s when millions of employees were not covered by a retirement plan at work. Most employers were simply unwilling or unable to contribute to pensions or profit sharing plans of any type. Nowadays, of course, many companies have popular 401(k) programs where contributions are made by both employers and eligible employees.

Initially, individuals could make tax-deductible IRA contributions (up to $1,500 annually) of 15 percent of earned income. There were 6 percent penalty taxes on excess contributions and 10 per cent penalty taxes on taxable withdrawals before $59^1/_2$; all account owners had to take at least minimum distributions at age $70^1/_2$ or pay a 50 percent penalty tax on the shortfall; and on "termination of employment" you could roll over all your money in an employer's qualified plan to an individual retirement account.

Today's (2003) IRA isn't much different from the original, traditional IRA. The 6 percent, 10 percent, and 50 percent penalty taxes still exist as do distributions at age $70^1/_2$. Rollovers are permitted (but today's rules are more liberal - see chapter 4). However, the deduction limits are higher, and there is a special non-deductible Roth IRA as well. Let me give you a picture of IRAs as they look at the present time:

(a) Contributions are up to the lesser of (a) 100 percent of compensation[1] annually, or (b) the contribution limit for the year ($3,000 in 2003-2004; $4,000 in 2005-2007; and $5,000 starting in 2008, with cost-of-living adjustments after 2008.) For individuals over age 50, an additional $500 is permitted during the years 2003-2005, and then an extra $1,000 between 2006-2010. A married person can contribute up to these amounts, as well, to an account for a non-working spouse. Of course, you can allocate your contributions between several traditional and Roth IRAs, if you wish.

A Comparison: In 1975, a married wage earner

---

1 Compensation now includes alimony paid under a divorce or separation agreement.

earning $10,000 or more could contribute only $1,500 to an IRA. In 2008, a married couple over age 50 (with one spouse earning $12,000) can contribute $12,000 ($6,000 for each spouse) - a big difference, indeed. Some think the limits on IRA contributions will move even higher[2] - especially if we have "self-directed" Social Security funding options someday.

(b) IRA deductions for allowable contributions to traditional IRAs as outlined in (a) above are reduced or completely eliminated if you participate in a qualified pension or profit sharing plan at work and your adjusted gross income (AGI) is too high,[3] or you are age $70^1/_2$. Any input that can't be deducted is referred to as a non-deductible contribution; - and this money can still be invested in the account without taxes on income or capital gains.[4] Contributions to Roths are also curbed or eliminated for high income taxpayers.

(c) Now, there are actually three types of IRAs - (i) a traditional account where deductions for contributions are permitted, and all withdrawals are taxable; (ii) a traditional account that includes non-deductible contributions; and (iii) Roths where there is no de-

2   Since tax reform seems to change constantly, Congress may even "move up" the limits on contributions. You could actually be able to contribute $6,000 in 2006 or even 2004.

3   For instance, a married participant earns $160,000 of compensation in 2002, 2003 or 2004; he or she can contribute $3,000 to an IRA, but no deduction is permitted.

4   Then, let's say a $100,000 traditional IRA (that includes non-deductible contributions of $5,000) is cashed-out after age $59^1/_2$. *The result:* $5,000 is tax-free, and $95,000 is taxable.

duction, and all withdrawals after age 59½ are tax-free if you've owned the account for five years.

(d) You can convert traditional IRAs to a Roth in a year when AGI is $100,000 or less - (see Chapter 2). Of course, the accumulation to-date is included in your taxable income for the conversion year.

(e) Eventually, the IRS forces you to "spend" the account. In 2002, the U.S. Treasury finally issued permanent regulations that cover taking minimum distributions at age 70½ - more about these in chapter 6.

The bottom line:[5] Over three decades, annual contributions to IRAs have increased markedly. And, since many account owners will surely roll-over their tax sheltered annuities (TSAs), pensions and 401(k) funds into an IRA (see Chapter 4) virtually all serious retirement money may someday be in self-managed individual retirement arrangements.

5   This is general information. To find out more about limits on IRA contributions and deductions, check with your financial advisor.

2.

Converting traditional IRAs to Roths

"People say I'm indecisive, but I don't know about that." George Bush

Of course, you can't deduct contributions to a Roth IRA. But, where else can you invest and earn fully tax-free returns on the money? Perhaps, (a) municipal bonds where the interest is tax-free, or (b) life insurance where one's cash value accumulation and the death benefit is also tax-free! True, but municipals generally pay less interest than taxable bonds, and if you cancel a life insurance policy the insurer will issue a form 1099 for any profit in the contract.

Roth accumulations (and post-$59^1/_2$ distributions after a five year period) are tax-free, period! These are appealing features in any long-term savings program. Roths have other benefits as well. For instance, you still can contribute to Roths after age $70^1/_2$. And, you needn't take any distributions ever from a Roth;[6] if you do, this isn't considered income, either, in calculating taxes on Social Security benefits.

Unfortunately, you can't contribute to a Roth if

6 **Note:** although you (or spouse) aren't required to take withdrawals from Roths, your beneficiaries must take at least minimum distributions over their lifetimes – or pay a 50 percent penalty tax on shortfalls.

your AGI is too high (see Chapter 1). But, you can convert (rollover) a traditional IRA to a Roth if AGI is $100,000 or less.

Aware of the Roth basics, you give a financial advisor these facts and objectives:

• You (age 60) have a $500,000 traditional IRA and anticipate AGI this year of $100,000 or less. (Or, you can create tax deductions or defer taxable income into the future to reduce current AGI to $100,000 at most).

• You like the idea of leaving a Roth to children and grandchildren where they can take tax-free distributions over a long period of time.

• There is probably enough money outside your present account to pay taxes on a conversion. In fact, you'd like to avoid taxes on the income that this capital currently earns.

Here is a report provided by the advisor:

A Roth Conversion Analysis

Let's say you pay income taxes at a 25 percent rate and can earn a 6 percent return on your investments. Consequently, you need $125,000 outside the IRA to pay taxes on a full $500,000 conversion.[7] Afterwards, you'll eliminate $7,500 in taxable income from the non-IRA tax capital. *The result:* Your $500,000 IRA is fully tax-paid and tax-free.[8]

7 Alternately, if you project a series of years when incomes will be $100,000 or less, you might gradually convert from the traditional IRA to a Roth. This could keep down marginal tax rates applied to the converted sums.

8 Actually, the law imposes a five-year period where only withdrawals up to today's value of $500,000 are tax-free.

The bottom line: The Roth conversion works well if distributions from a traditional IRA and income from the tax capital would be taxed at the same (or higher) rate than your tax rate at point of conversion. *The reason:* You replace taxable income outside the IRA with tax-free income inside the IRA.

The proof: Assume (a) a minimum distribution of $30,000 from the traditional IRA - 6 percent of $500,000, (b) $7,500 in interest from non-IRA investments, and (c) a 25 percent income tax rate. You'd pay $9,375 in taxes on $37,500 and the net would be $28,125. Instead, if you convert to a Roth and take 6 percent tax-free ($30,000) from the account, you'll net a full $30,000 - an improvement of $1,875. Tax magic, you say; that's correct.

If you will be in a low tax bracket - say, merely 10 percent at retirement, the conversion probably doesn't make sense. In the above example, you'd pay taxes of $3,750 on $37,500 - and have a net of $33,750; If you did convert, you'd have merely $30,000 from the Roth.

An added bonus: After the conversion, if you can live comfortably on non-IRA capital, and don't withdraw from the Roth, it can build tax-free as long as you and your spouse are alive. For example, a $500,000 Roth earning six percent compounded annually will grow to $2 million over a 24 year period. That's quite a kitty to leave to family. And, you can always take withdrawals in an emergency.

Sincerely yours,

Your Advisor

In summary, if you have a significant traditional IRA, consider a Roth conversion - especially if you have the tax capital and are willing to pay the IRS up-front.

3.

Gifting to a grandchild's IRA

"Blessed are the young for they shall inherit the national debt."
Herbert Hoover

Sometimes, I'm asked about gifts that assure the financial security of someone's child or grandchild. Well, you can't do much better than adding money to a grandchild's IRA. Here's why:

Let's assume your talented 16-year-old grandson, Tommy, earns about $3,000 per year working odd jobs - and, he either spends this money or sets it aside for college education and expenses. Since Tommy's earnings are clearly "compensation" under the law, you think he should take advantage of an IRA program. Yet, (a) Tommy really can't afford to part with the money, and (b) a tax deduction for contributions to a traditional IRA wouldn't be of much value anyway. Voila! Perhaps you could make gifts to a tax-free Roth IRA that would be helpful when he retires.

Note: You may think that a wage earner must use his or her money to make an IRA contribution. However, the IRS has determined that the source of funds contributed is immaterial so long as the wage earner has compensation at least equal to the contribution.

You make some calculations assuming the Roth could earn six percent consistently. *The conclusion:* If there were $3,000 contributions to Tommy's Roth for each of the next five years, he would have about $250,000 on-hand at age 65; an eight percent return would give him over $560,000. What a great idea. It's too good to pass up.

After meetings with Mary (Tommy's mother) and a financial planner, you have a thoughtful conversation with your grandson. Here's what you tell him:

"I've decided to deposit $3,000 into a special account[9] called a Roth IRA UFGMA; your mother will be custodian for your benefit until adulthood. My plan is to add at least four more annual contributions. Just tell me each year what your wages are because I can't contribute more than you earn.

"The beneficiary now will be 'your estate,' but in time the recipient can be someone you select.

"This is a program for later in life where there may be several hundred thousand dollars you can enjoy at retirement. However, the money will always be there earlier in an emergency; just know you'll pay taxes and probably a 10 percent penalty too, on anything withdrawn before age $59^1/_2$.

"Even though this account is for retirement, you still needn't take anything out, ever. And, if you don't,

9   This will be an account titled "Mary, custodian, under the Uniform Gifts to Minors Act (UFGMA), in _____," Tommy's state of residence.

there will be more in the account to grow tax-free. Consequently, if there are other assets you can count on, spend these if possible. The IRA will be something you can leave to family as well, and they'll also receive it *tax-free*. And Tommy, if Congress were to modify the tax law, your account should be protected from any unfavorable changes."

He is really pleased. You are ecstatic. What a great way to do something for the next generation.

Here are a few additional items to remember:

• Tommy can always establish another traditional or Roth IRA and contribute to it over the years. *Be aware:* Total contributions (his and yours) to his IRAs should never exceed overall limits in the law (see Chapter 1).

• Under the UFGMA, the Roth account will be turned over to Tommy officially the year he is considered an adult, as actually defined by state law.

• Of course, you can make other gifts to Tommy as well. One possibility is an annual premium-transfer into a life insurance contract on his life. Withdrawals from the policy are tax-free, as well, and the company can't cancel the policy if he is in poor health later in life. Gifts into insurance policies aren't subject to IRA compensation requirements or limits on contributions either.

In summary, gifts into a grandchild's Roth are a fine thing to do. This is serious money that just keeps giving in return.

And to think he inherits my IRA!

4.

Rolling tax-deferred money over to an IRA

"The avoidance of taxes is the only intellectual pursuit that carries any reward." John Maynard Keynes

There are a number of situations in which distributions from a retirement plan must be included in your taxable income. It's here that the law permits a "second-look" before you pay taxes on this money. Let me explain:

If you receive "some or all of the balance to your credit" from an employer's qualified retirement plan (usually, when you terminate employment or retire), you can roll over all or a portion to an IRA. *The result:* What would otherwise be taxable becomes tax-sheltered once more. You also gain control of the funds and may have more investment choices within the IRA. Finally, if you kept everything in the qualified plan, a beneficiary may only be permitted a lump sum at your death that is fully taxable in a single year.

Be aware: Even though the reasons to rollover look compelling, there still can be advantages to keeping the money in a qualified plan. For instance, IRAs cannot invest in life insurance; qualified plans can acquire life policies, and even tax sheltered annuities (TSAs) can purchase retirement income life contracts. An IRA cannot make a tax-free loan; a qualified plan can make certain loans that aren't taxable to a participant. And, IRAs cannot invest in art, stamps and coins; while a 401(k) account may acquire these investments.

Here are some interesting rollover possibilities:

• You receive a payment from your spouse's qualified retirement plan or IRA based on a qualified domestic relations order (QDRO); this can be rolled to your personal IRA.

• You own a TSA. And, you are either (a) terminating employment, (b) disabled under the law, or (c) at least age $59^1/_2$. If you want more control of the TSA's investments, you roll it to an IRA. *Step one:* Ask the insurer for the policy's cash value. *Step two:* Within 60 days of receipt, roll the cash into your IRA. (Or, ask the insurance company to make a direct transfer of cash value to this IRA.)

• You take money from an IRA; this can be rolled to another IRA (only once in any one-year period), or even to a new qualified plan at work.

• A surviving spouse who is sole beneficiary can roll their mate's IRA or qualified plan account to a personal IRA. (See Chapter 8 for more information on spousal rollovers.)

Rollovers can be divided among several IRAs if you wish. And if your employer's qualified plan accepts rollovers, you can transfer an IRA directly to that program.

Warning: Once you receive a distribution eligible for a rollover, you must complete the transaction within 60 calendar days. If you receive more than one distribution, the 60 days applies to each payment. You cannot rollover a distribution into another person's IRA.[10]

Another word of caution: Since there is a mandatory 20 percent income tax withheld on distributions from qualified plans (but not IRAs), *you must add this tax to your rollover.* Otherwise, you have to pay income tax on the tax withheld and possibly a 10 percent penalty tax as well.

Example: You receive $100,000 from an employer's profit sharing plan, and $20,000 in taxes are withheld. Within 60 calendar days, you rollover the net distribution of $80,000. *The result:* You still owe income taxes on $20,000;[11] if you are under age 59$^{1}/_{2}$, there may also be a $2,000 (10 percent) penalty. (See Chapter 5.) *The solution:* Ask your employer to transfer $100,000 directly to the IRA, instead. (Alternately, if you have another $20,000 to spare, add it

10 This is clear from a case in which someone received a distribution from a qualified plan. And, he placed these funds in a traditional IRA in his wife's name within 60 days. It didn't work; he paid income taxes on the distribution.
11 *The reason:* The law also considers the $20,000 in taxes a distribution subject to taxes.

to the $80,000 rollover. The employer's $20,000 paid to the IRS will simply count toward your tax obligation on other taxable income for the year.)

In the next chapter, I'll discuss what happens when you take "premature" distributions from an IRA that are not rolled back into the account.

5.

When you need money before age 59¹/₂

"Thank heavens we don't get all the government we pay for."
Will Rogers

In chapter 1, I mention a 10 percent penalty on taxable IRA withdrawals made prior to age 59¹/₂. The purpose of the penalty is to discourage taking money before retirement. It has been in the law since 1974 when IRAs began. Still, your IRA remains available in a crisis for emergencies where other assets shouldn't be spent, or times when it isn't convenient to tap a line of credit.

(Actually, those who withdraw IRA money before age 59¹/₂ will probably not have much income, and they'll likely be in a low tax bracket - or perhaps no tax bracket - in the year they take the money. A 10 percent tax added to a 10 percent tax or so really isn't very much anyway. But, if someone takes the IRA distribution and can work around the tax penalty, why not!)

In fairness to taxpayers, the law allows a few exceptions to the 10 percent tax. For instance, there is no penalty on IRA payments -

- if you are the beneficiary of a deceased IRA owner;
- if you are disabled;
- for your medical expenses, after 7.5 percent of adjusted gross income is subtracted;
- for an unemployed IRA owner's health insurance premiums;
- for certain family higher education expenses;
- to build, buy, or rebuild your first home (up to $10,000); and
- of distributions that represent non-deductible contributions. Let's say in 2008, you earned more than $5,000 and were permitted a $5,000 IRA contribution; but, because of your participation in a pension plan at work, you could only deduct $2,000. Consequently, a $3,000 non-deductible amount is carried forward within your traditional IRA. Later, you liquidate this account before age $59\frac{1}{2}$. *The result:* After subtracting $3,000, the balance is subject to a 10 percent penalty.

If you can't qualify under these exceptions, here's a way to avoid the tax:

At age 55, assume you have a financial emergency and need $30,000. Your first thought is to take this money from your $100,000 traditional IRA. After a conference with a financial planner, you receive this advice:

• Obtain a bank loan for $30,000. You'll owe six annual installments of $6,500 including interest - a payback of $39,000.

• Calculate the payment you'd receive if your full $100,000 IRA were systematically paid out as an "annuity" over your 30-year IRS life expectancy. Let's say this is also $6,500 annually - a total anticipated payout of $195,000. These $6,500 payments are the same as the installments you owe the bank.

• Once the six year bank loan is repaid (at your age 61), you'll be past age $59\frac{1}{2}$ and can cease taking taxable payments from the IRA.

The result: You'll owe income taxes on each $6,500 IRA distribution, but there will be no extra 10 percent penalty tax to pay.

The bottom line: Before taking early IRA distributions, know whether you can protect IRA withdrawals from the 10% tax. If not, you can always use the systematic payment rule to sidestep this tax.

We can get cash out of your IRA,
can't we?

6.

Surprise! It's payout time at age 70 $^1/_2$

"There are three signs of old age: Loss of memory...
I forget the other two." Red Skelton

As IRAs enter a fourth decade, they have become "something to look forward to" in uncertain times. The ideas of (a) a regular tax deduction for paying yourself first, (b) legally avoiding taxes as the account builds up, and (c) tax-free rollovers to an account that you control, are refreshing concepts indeed. Traditional IRA's are surely the centerpiece to most sound retirement planning.

But, let's say in your 60s you become aware that at age 70$^1/_2$ there will be no more deductible IRA contributions, and minimum distributions will just increase your taxable income. You may prefer to keep everything intact and simply let beneficiaries pay taxes on the account someday, I'm not surprised.

Let me help put these IRA distributions at age 70$^1/_2$ in perspective:

Example: In your 60s, you are married and plan

on a $500,000 traditional IRA about the time you reach age 70¹/₂. Let's assume that joint tax rates are simply 30 percent.

One approach is to simply cash-out the $500,000 account at age 70¹/₂ and pay $150,000 or so in income taxes. You'll have $350,000 to reinvest and no concerns about future IRA distributions issues. (Alternately, if your adjusted gross income is $100,000 or less, you might convert to a Roth where minimum distributions aren't required and everything can be tax-free thereafter.)

But, since the idea of paying $150,000 in taxes "up front," doesn't seem appealing, you investigate taking out IRA distributions as slowly as possible under the law. Here's what you discover:

At age 70¹/₂, the first required annual distribution must be around four percent[12] of the account's value (presumably, $500,000) - or about $20,000. The balance ($480,000) can grow tax-free in your IRA. In fact, the IRS requirement on minimum IRA distributions doesn't even reach eight percent until you turn age 89. Assume you take only minimum amounts each year and the IRA continues to build at say, eight percent annually after age 70¹/₂. *The result at 89:* The account will actually be worth about $800,000. That's 160 percent of the $500,000 you had 18 years

12 See Exhibits A and B at the end of this chapter. To determine minimum withdrawals, divide the account's value on December 31st of the previous year by your current life expectancy in the Uniform Lifetime Table in Exhibit A; or, multiply this sum by the corresponding percentage in Exhibit B.

earlier when you were 70$^1/_2$.

My advice: Make some projections in your 60's, and build a distributions model based on the IRS required minimums after age 70$^1/_2$. This sound financial planning assures optimum tax deferral within your account and usually works out best.

Another possibility: Assume at age 70$^1/_2$, you have a $500,000 non-IRA fund invested in taxable bonds paying interest of about $25,000 annually. And, you really don't need the $20,000 or so that IRS forces you to take from the IRA. When the taxable IRA payments begin, convert your $500,000 non-IRA kitty into tax-free or tax-deferred capital such as municipals, deferred annuities, single premium life insurance, or unimproved real estate. That way, as IRA taxable distributions begin, the non-IRA taxable income ceases. Makes sense, doesn't it!

Exhibit A

IRS Uniform Lifetime Table (ages 70-115+)

Age of IRA Owner	Distrib. Period (Years)	Age of IRA Owner	Distrib. Period (Years)	Age of IRA Owner	Distrib. Period (Years)
70	27.4	85	14.8	100	6.3
71	26.5	86	14.1	101	5.9
72	25.6	87	13.4	102	5.5
73	24.7	88	12.7	103	52
74	23.8	89	12.0	104	4.9
75	22.9	90	11.4	105	4.5
76	22.0	91	10.8	106	4.2
77	21.2	92	10.2	107	3.9
78	20.3	93	9.6	108	3.7
79	19.5	94	9.1	109	3.4
80	18.7	95	8.6	110	3.1
81	17.9	96	8.1	111	2.9
82	17.1	97	7.6	112	2.6
83	16.3	98	7.1	113	2.4
84	15.5	99	6.7	114	2.1
				115+	1.9

Exhibit B

IRS Uniform Lifetime Table

(converted to percentages)[13]

Age of IRA Owner	Required Minimum Distrib. Percent	Age of IRA Owner	Required Minimum Distrib. Percent	Age of IRA Owner	Required Minimum Distrib. Percent
70	3.6496	85	6.7567	100	15.8730
71	3.7736	86	7.0921	101	16.9492
72	3.9062	87	7.4626	102	18.1818
73	4.0485	88	7.8740	103	19.2308
74	4.2016	89	8.3333	104	20.4082
75	4.3668	90	8.7719	105	22.2222
76	4.5455	91	9.2592	106	23.8095
77	4.7169	92	9.8039	107	25.6410
78	4.9261	93	10.4166	108	27.0270
79	5.1282	94	10.9890	109	29.4118
80	5.3475	95	11.6279	110	32.2581
81	5.5865	96	12.3457	111	34.4483
82	5.8479	97	13.1579	112	38.4615
83	6.1349	98	14.1845	113	41.6667
84	6.4516	99	14.9254	114	47.6190
				115+	52.6316

13 See Exhibit A, and for each age divide 1 by life expectancy to obtain the required minimum distribution percentage.

The Lifetime Table says I've only got 3 weeks
to go. Why not have fun?

7.

Getting serious about your IRA beneficiary designation

"I am prepared to meet my Maker. Whether my Maker is prepared for the ordeal of meeting me is another matter." Winston Churchill

It should be no surprise that IRA beneficiary designations pre-empt instructions in a will that specify who will receive this money someday. Consequently, an IRA simply passes according to custodial paperwork which could be incorrect, out-of-date, or simply out-of-mind. Let me explain:

Here are primary[14] beneficiaries most people name on IRA set-up forms.

(a) An individual - husband, wife, child, grandchild, parent or other friend or relative.

(b) A group of people, - for instance:

• "My children equally." Be aware that this designation disinherits the children (your grandchildren)

---

14 A *primary* beneficiary inherits at an account owner's death, a *contingent* beneficiary inherits if there is no available primary recipient, and a *successor* beneficiary inherits what's left after the first beneficiary dies.

of a child who predeceases you. *The reason:* If there are children still alive, the deceased child's portion just increases their shares.

• "My issue, *per stirpes.*" This leaves a deceased child's share to his or her children who "come-up" to receive it.

(c) A charity.

(d) "My estate." This enables an IRA to pass according to the will.

(e) "A living trust in existence at my death." The account simply becomes one of the trust's assets.

(f) "A trust under my will." The IRA becomes a trust asset when your estate's   representative opens a trust account.

Unfortunately, since many IRA owners pay precious little attention to their beneficiary designation, there can be a number of traps and surprises for the unwary. Here are a few:

(a) *Naming "my estate" beneficiary.* This designation allows an estate's creditors to attach the account.[15] Consider this example: You own two assets - a $100,000 bank account and a $300,000 IRA payable to your estate - a total of $400,000. You also have $200,000 in personal debts when you die. *The result:* Your family nets $200,000 ($400,000 less $200,000). If a creditor-protected IRA names a

---

15 There is also an income tax disadvantage. Since "my estate" is not an individual with a life expectancy, the law requires a cash-out of the IRA within five years after death.

spouse or children beneficiary, your estate's claimant would be entitled to only the $100,000 in the bank account, leaving your family $300,000 net.

(b) *Failure to specify a contingent beneficiary.* If the first (primary) designee predeceases you, a contingent beneficiary becomes the primary recipient. If none, the IRA bounces over to your estate. (See (a) above.)

(c) *Failure to specify a successor (secondary) beneficiary.* Let's say you name a daughter, Nancy, primary recipient of the account. (Her son, Tommy, is the contingent beneficiary.) After inheriting your IRA, Nancy dies without naming a new (successor) beneficiary. *The result:* Since Tommy was only a beneficiary if Nancy predeceased you, the account now passes to Nancy's estate. *The solution:* Name a successor to receive the IRA if Nancy fails to specify a subsequent beneficiary.

(d) *Naming minor children beneficiaries.* Their shares will be managed by a court appointed guardian, possibly even in-laws or strangers. Assume that Bobby, a divorced son, predeceases you and your IRA passes to his children. If they are not adults, his estranged wife or her parents will probably have control of the account. The likely solution: A trust to benefit your grandchildren.

(e) *Not including a beneficiary's spouse in the planning.* When naming beneficiaries, we tend to think in terms of blood relatives (children, grandchildren, great-grandchildren, etc.) *The result:* A deceased heir's widow or widower can be left out of this picture. If so, it's possible he or she must work just to make ends meet. *The solution:* A trust-beneficiary for your IRA that provides income for spouses of deceased heirs - at least for a period of time.

(f) *Being careless with wording on the beneficiary form.* If your beneficiary is "my children," an illegitimate child would surely receive an equal share. If you want different shares for different folks, your lawyer will surely have to draft the wording.

(g) *Not updating the beneficiary form.* Truly, the only thing that stays the same is change. We marry, have children, divorce, remarry and inherit second families. We also get into financial trouble, become ill and die. *The problem:* If IRA beneficiary forms aren't updated regularly, it's possible the account will someday belong to a former spouse, unfriendly creditors, or those who can't manage the money. *The solution:* When things change, adjust beneficiary designations to fit the circumstances.

8.

Leave an IRA directly to your spouse

"I haven't spoken to my wife in years - I didn't want to interrupt her."
Rodney Dangerfield

In chapter 7, I explain the importance of selecting an IRA beneficiary. Of course, if married, you'll likely name your spouse first recipient (and children for any residue after you are both gone). The beneficiary form might read like this:

Primary beneficiary - "My wife (Mary)."

Contingent beneficiary - "If Mary doesn't survive me, to my children in equal shares."

Successor beneficiary - "If Mary does survive me, any balance at her death passes to my children in equal shares."

Warning: As I caution in chapter 10, IRA custodians vary greatly in their approach to providing assistance and alternatives for account owners. Don't take anything for granted. Discuss beneficiary designations with your attorney and financial advisor before deciding on what to do.

When Mary receives your IRA, she'll either keep the account as is (an *inherited IRA*) or retitle it in her name (a *rollover IRA*).

1. An "inherited IRA," where she keeps everything in your name

If Mary keeps your account intact, the law provides that -

• if she is under age 59$^1/_2$ and takes a withdrawal, there is no 10 percent penalty tax;

• if you died before age 70$^1/_2$, she needn't take distributions until *April 1st following the year* **you** *would have reached age 70$^1/_2$.* Thereafter, required minimum distributions will be based on her redetermined IRS life expectancy[16] each year;

• if your custodian permits, Mary can name the successor beneficiary; and

• a successor beneficiary must use Mary's fixed remaining life expectancy to calculate any required minimum distributions in the future.

Here is an example that makes this more clear:

You were born October 1, 1936, and die in 2002 at age 66; Mary is 62. If you had lived to age 70$^1/_2$ in 2007, Mary would be 67. The result: She must begin taking distributions in 2008 when her IRS life expectancy at 68 is 18.6 years.[17] Her first minimum payment will be 5.3764 percent (1 ÷ .186) of the account's balance on December 31, 2007. She'll redetermine her IRS life expectancy (17.8, 17.0, and 16.3 years, respectively, etc.) in following years to deter-

16 Each year, her IRS life expectancy is projected (redetermined based on her age in that year). Then, at her death, a remaining life expectancy is determined (fixed), and one full year is subtracted annually until the account is completely spent.

17 See the IRS unisex life expectancy table (Exhibit A) at the end of this chapter.

mine the minimum portion she must withdraw from your account.

Now, let's say Mary dies at age 85 when her IRS life expectancy is 7.6 years. A successor beneficiary must take at least minimum amounts based on Mary's fixed remaining lifespan (6.6, 5.6, and 4.6, years, respectively, etc.) beginning in the year after her death.

2. A rollover of your account to an IRA in her name

Alternately, Mary can rollover your IRA by simply retitling it in her name where the law provides -

• If she is under age $59^1/_2$ and takes a withdrawal, the 10 percent penalty tax rules still are applicable.

• She needn't take distributions until *April 1st following the year **she** is actually age $70^1/_2$.* Her required minimum distributions will also be based on the IRS Uniform Lifetime Table. (See Chapter 6, which combines her IRS life expectancy and the lifespan of a fictional person 10 years younger.)

• Since Mary is now the account owner, she can name a new beneficiary who can take minimum amounts based on his or her personal IRS life expectancy at Mary's death.

Let's use the facts in the inherited IRA example and see what effect a rollover has on Mary's required minimum distributions from her rollover IRA:

You die in 2002 at age 66 when Mary is 62. She must begin taking distributions nine years later

(2011) at age 71. Then, the Uniform Lifetime Table uses a divisor of 26.5 to determine her first minimum distribution [a percentage of 3.7736 (1 ÷ .265)] of the account's balance on December 31, 2010. She redetermines her lifespan using this table (25.6, 24.7, and 23.8 years respectively, etc.) to calculate minimum distribution percentages in years thereafter (3.9062%, 4.0485%, 4.2016%, etc.).

Now, let's say Mary dies at age 85 (when her actual IRS life expectancy is only 7.6 years), and her primary beneficiary is her great-grandson, Tommy age seven. Tommy can take distributions from Mary's account over the next 74.8 years. (See Exhibit A in Chapter 13.) If you compare this to an "inherited" account,[18] Mary's rollover wins hands down when it comes to required minimum distributions after she dies. *The reason:* Once she rollsover the account, her primary beneficiary (Tommy) can always use his life expectancy to determine his payout.

The bottom line: A traditional IRA is just a bundle of money awaiting taxes charged by the system. If you are married, it pays to understand that in most cases a surviving spouse who receives an IRA directly will rollover the account. And, although the law always permits unlimited distributions from an IRA, the trick will be to know *how little* to take without incurring the 50 percent penalty tax. (See Chapter 6.) Then, if the spouse doesn't have to take any more, he

---

18 If Mary doesn't roll over the account, Tommy must take distributions over only her 7.6 year remaining life expectancy.

or she continues with a minimum distributions/optimum tax deferral plan that a beneficiary can maintain after his or her death.

Exhibit A

IRS unisex single life expectancies - ages 56-111+

Age of IRA Owner Or Designated Beneficiary	Expectancy (Years)	Age of IRA Owner Or Designated Beneficiary	Expectancy (Years)
56	28.7	84	8.1
57	27.9	85	7.6
58	27.0	86	7.1
59	26.1	87	6.7
60	25.2	88	6.3
61	24.4	89	5.9
62	23.5	90	5.5
63	22.7	91	5.2
64	21.8	92	4.9
65	21.0	93	4.6
66	20.2	94	4.3
67	19.4	95	4.1
68	18.6	96	3.8
69	17.8	97	3.6
70	17.0	98	3.4
71	16.3	99	3.1
72	15.5	100	2.9
73	14.8	101	2.7
74	14.1	102	2.5
75	13.4	103	2.3
76	12.7	104	2.1
77	12.1	105	1.9
78	11.4	106	1.7
79	10.8	107	1.5
80	10.2	108	1.4
81	9.7	109	1.2
82	9.1	110	1.1
83	8.6	111+	1.0

9.

Leave an IRA to benefit your spouse – an "IRA trust"

"If love is the answer, could you rephrase the question?" Lily Tomlin

In chapter 8, I observe that most married account owners will leave their IRA directly to a spouse and then to children. On receipt, the surviving spouse treats the account as an inherited IRA. Or, she rolls it over to a personal IRA which significantly slows minimum distributions requirements in the law; the next beneficiary can always use his or her life expectancy to calculate minimum payments after the spouse dies.

The issue: If your spouse isn't comfortable investing large sums of money or falls prey to creditors or unscrupulous persons, it's possible everything you've worked so hard to save could be lost. *Another word of caution:* A spouse-beneficiary may select new beneficiaries; perhaps children from another marriage, a new mate, or even a paramour. If you aren't comfortable with these possibilities, name an IRA trust[19] re-

---

19 In most cases, this will be a qualified terminable interest property (QTIP) trust. A QTIP trust gives a spouse the use of trust assets while alive. Thereafter, everything passes according to wording in the document.

cipient for the benefit of your spouse.

You'll recall that the IRS wants all IRA owners to take minimum distributions beginning at age $70^1/_2$. It also wants those who inherit accounts - even trustees - to take minimum lifetime distributions as well. And, since only individuals have life expectancies, there are some special requirements for trustees to qualify as "individual" beneficiaries.

For instance, your IRA trust must be valid under state law and irrevocable at your death. (Of course, this enables a revocable living trust that becomes final when the trust creator dies to qualify under the rules.) All trust beneficiaries must be clearly identifiable, and trust paperwork delivered to the IRA custodian or administrator by October 31st of the year following death. Finally, required minimum distributions are based on the oldest trust beneficiary's life expectancy.

This is just the beginning when considering an IRA trust for your spouse.

A lot depends on the language in the document. It determines, for instance, whether the plan qualifies the account's value for an estate tax marital deduction. (If so, she'll have a right to all income earned by the account, even if this exceeds the minimum distribution required by law.) It also establishes just how much the trustee must take each year (and whether this or even more must systematically be paid over to your spouse).

Let's assume your spouse Mary, is age 71 at your death when an account is left to her IRA marital trust. It's possible that the future minimum distributions will be based on one of the following: Her fixed IRS life expectancy at age 72 of 15.5 years (see Chapter 8), her 15.5- year life expectancy that is redetermined annually, or even a 26.5-year fictitious life expectancy (see Chapter 6) a figure that is redetermined annually. Obviously, the latter - based on the longest life expectancy (and largest divisors) - imposes the smallest payments from the account. Everything depends on how the trust is written. In general, if Mary has more control over it, she'll have a lower required distribution.

The bottom line: If you want an optimum tax deferral plan, make a transfer directly to your spouse. If you want maximum control over the account, however, an IRA marital trust is better. Get good advice. Without it, your IRA just might die with you.

10.

Continuing the plan – optimum tax deferral for generations-to-come

"The reason grandparents and grandchildren get along so well is that they have a common enemy." Sam Levinson

In chapter 6, I advance the concepts of (a) taking minimum IRA distributions at age $70^1/_2$, and (b) leaving maximum value in the account directly to someone to build thereafter.

In this segment, I'll discuss how to continue this program for the next generation and perhaps the next. This plan works best when you have other assets for a spouse or aren't married.

Example: Let's say at age $70^1/_2$ you take only minimum distributions under the law as the remaining balance presumably earns 8 percent annually. *The result:* The rate of earnings significantly outpaces the rate of withdrawals. By your 89th birthday, your account will be worth nearly $800,000 - the point at which the minimum distributions percentage increases to 8.33 percent. Then, the balance on hand will begin to diminish because the rate of withdrawal (more than 8 percent) exceeds the assumed rate of return (8 percent). You die. Your beneficiary's age and life expectancy now control the minimum distributions required by law, which automatically changes the payout calculations.

Assume your beneficiary is a great-grandson, Tommy, age seven and that his IRS life expectancy is 75.8 years (See Exhibit A in chapter 13). When he turns eight (and his IRS life expectancy is 74.8 years), he takes a first required minimum distribution of $10,695 which is 1.3369 percent of $800,000. *Here's the proof:* (1 ÷ .748 equals 1.3369). At age nine, he'll take 1.3550 percent (1 ÷ .738); at 10, he'll take 1.3736 percent (1 ÷ .728); etc.

Your successor beneficiary can continue the plan based on a formula that takes into account Tommy's life expectancy remaining at his death. Assume Tommy dies at age 67, 60 years after commencing distributions from your IRA. Since his life expectancy is 15.8 years (which is what remains when you subtract those 60 years from his original 75.8-year life expectancy), the next year the next beneficiary can take 6.7568 percent (1 ÷ .148). Then, 7.2464 percent (1 ÷ .138), 7.8125 percent (1 ÷ .128), 8.4746 percent (1 ÷ .118); etc.

The bottom line: It's just good planning to defer taxes as long as possible. If you are interested in this approach, here are 10 more planning pointers to consider:

1. You need to be careful about beneficiary designations. (Although you can change the designee as desired, keep everything up-to-date.) If you want to stretch the payments, remember that you always need an individual beneficiary on the account. "My estate" doesn't have a life expectancy, and is therefore not an individual beneficiary.

2. When naming a beneficiary, work closely with your IRA custodian-provider. *Be aware:* Most providers answer questions via a toll-free number using trained staff. But, they have carefully prepared scripts and aren't always able to deal with tailored beneficiary designations. In most cases, they aren't equipped to determine a series of required minimum distributions either.

3. In our example, Tommy is age seven and therefore a minor by law. Until he reaches adulthood, a guardian or trustee must take Tommy's distributions from your IRA.

4. Who is this person or organization likely to be? If Tommy's parent (your child) divorces or dies while Tommy is still a child, it's possible your child's divorced spouse or in-law will be in charge of your IRA.

5. If Tommy's parents are alive, you might leave the IRA outright to them instead. They can pass what's left to Tommy eventually. Of course, a parent's life expectancy is shorter, causing smaller divisors and larger distributions from the account.

6. If there are several grandchildren (or grandchildren and children), you can divide an IRA into separate accounts, one for each individual beneficiary.

7. A required minimum distribution is exactly that; a beneficiary can always take more.

8. If a child or grandchild is divorced or not capable of managing investments (or if you are concerned about a beneficiary taking excessive amounts from the account), it's possible to substitute trusts as IRA beneficiaries for them. There should probably be one beneficiary per trust to make clear whose life expectancy determines the minimum distributions.

9. Minimum distributions planning works especially well if there is emergency capital outside the IRA or your beneficiary has earned income to meet personal needs. Take these factors into account when arranging a stretch-like minimum distribution plan for your heirs.

10. Finally, you'll recall that in Chapter 8, I discussed the possibility that your spouse as a direct IRA beneficiary, can rollover the account. Then, as a part of the plan, her beneficiaries can use their IRS life expectancies to stretch-out distributions after she dies.[20]

In summary, if optimum tax deferral is your goal, arrange a minimum distributions program. If pos-

20 Note the differences. When a spouse-beneficiary rolls over the account, her beneficiaries use their personal life expectancies eventually. Other primary beneficiaries cannot rollover the account; consequently, their successors must continue using what remains of the primary designee's life expectancy at death.

sible, divide the account into separate IRAs and name younger beneficiaries (who will have longer life expectancies, larger divisors and smaller minimums). Since each beneficiary can always take greater withdrawals, there really is nothing to lose. Of course, you might name trusts as beneficiaries instead. Then, the trust document will spell out what is paid to everyone.

11.

IRAs in a second marriage

"Marriage is a great institution, but I'm not ready for an institution."
Mae West

Here's the situation. You and your spouse, Karen, have children from previous marriages. You want her to receive income from a $400,000 traditional IRA while alive, while preserving at least $200,000 for each of your two children.

You know that if Karen inherits the IRA directly, she'll surely assume control and name her children to receive what remains when she dies. But if you leave it to a trust for her (and your children next), there probably won't be much left for them anyway (after the trustee passes on to Karen any distributions taken from your account).

Observation: Contrast this with a first marriage where you'd probably leave the account directly to Karen, trusting her to preserve what's left for any children.

I recommend the following arrangements to achieve equitable results:

(A) Leave the $400,000 account directly to Karen,

and purchase life insurance of $400,000 payable to your two children equally.

• Tell Karen she'll be free to name her children IRA beneficiary at her death. This clears the air.

• If you have impaired health (and higher premiums), discuss matters with your children; perhaps they'll help with the cost to protect their inheritance.

• Actually, you shouldn't have to acquire a $400,000 insurance policy. Since the $400,000 IRA is probably worth less after taxes, $300,000 in tax-paid insurance is more like the IRA's true value.

(B) Alternately, leave the account directly to your children, and purchase a life insurance policy payable to Karen.

• If a regular life policy is too costly, you might acquire an inexpensive reversionary annuity for Karen. This is also a life insurance policy, but it has no face amount; instead, it merely pays her a regular stipend that begins when you die and ceases at her death. For instance, this policy might pay a $2,000 monthly income which is roughly equivalent to a six percent return on a $400,000 lump sum.

• When you purchase traditional life insurance or a reversionary annuity for Karen, and leave an IRA to others, your attorney may suggest a post-marital agreement that clarifies your intentions. It may also be necessary to modify a pre-marital document if it provides otherwise. Certainly, Karen should seek legal counsel, as well, to monitor what's going on.

The moral to the story: In second marriages, everything changes. Obviously, husband and wife will desire financial security for each other. But, it's natural for each to want their assets to be available for their own children from a previous marriage. A solution that "replaces" an IRA with life insurance is both logical and emotionally appealing. It's best if both spouses discuss matters openly with spouse, counsel and financial advisors. That's the right thing to do.

I thought the IRA money was going to MY kids!

12.

IRA annuities –
how to take out your money

"You can live to be a hundred, if you give up all the things that make you want to be a hundred." Woody Allen

I'm sure you've heard the one about a friend who made a deal and got an "annuity" in return. *Translation:* A very desirable financial transaction where someone gets an income "perpetually," or at least for as long as they live. This explanation comes close to the classic definition of an annuity where someone receives a lifetime income from an insurance company (or payments for a set number of years).

Your financial adviser is apt to describe an annuity as a policy which credits interest that remains untaxed until distributed or withdrawn - this is an *accumulation annuity.* Of course, this policy can be "annuitized" eventually and make payments systematically as long as the annuitant lives - this is a *payout annuity. Example:* John Martin, age 65, invested $100,000 in an accumulation annuity that grew to $200,000. He annuitizes and receives a payout annuity of $1,400 monthly over 20 years guaranteed (or his lifetime, if longer).

When it comes to IRAs, annuities have been a relatively uncommon investment.[21] In 1999, $2.5 trillion dollars were held in IRAs but only $245 billion of these funds were managed directly by life insurance companies; most IRA funds were held by mutual funds, stock brokerage firms and other financial institutions instead. I believe this is about to change. Here's why:

• Although most states have laws that safeguard IRAs from creditors of account owners and beneficiaries, at least one court has cast doubt on the extent of this protection. Meanwhile, two-thirds of the states provide separate creditor protection for annuities. That's why I think it is wise for an IRA owner to enhance asset protection by acquiring annuities for her account.

• Insurers are fairly creative in designing their accumulation annuity contracts. For instance, you can get policies that guarantee fixed current returns, say five percent per annum, so-called *fixed annuities*. The same insurers typically may guarantee three percent, but give upside returns that depend on a stock market index - an *equity index annuity*. Or, a company may offer an unlimited upside (but an unlimited downside as well) - *a variable annuity*. The industry

---

21 One of the reasons is that some advisors believe it is improper to acquire a tax-deferred investment (a non-qualified accumulation annuity) in an account that is already tax-deferred (an IRA). As annuities become more "user-friendly" in IRAs, this notion will change.

is changing and will do even better for consumers in the future. Look for competitive product enhancements especially with indexed and variable policies.

• Under the law, IRA owners are forced to take distributions over life expectancies in effect at age $70^1/_2$. Payout annuities are a natural way to complete this process. *What's more:* We are living longer and naturally want the security of incomes that can't be outlived; insurance companies provide this assurance.

• In 2002, the IRS issued regulations that approve certain payout annuities in IRAs. Insurers are encouraged to give consumers more annuitizing options. (I predict the industry will react creatively to this "nudge.")

Let me describe an IRA annuity that I am sure you will be able to purchase shortly:

Example: Bob Morgan is in his 50s or 60s and is aware that at age $70^1/_2$ he'll have to begin the IRA liquidation process. Bob's IRA acquires an accumulation annuity policy that pays either (a) a fixed rate of return, (b) a minimum rate plus an equity indexed upside, or (c) a variable rate based on the performance of a group of mutual funds. He can mix these and change selections at least annually. His policy information is also coded and available on-line.

Bob's insurer will calculate minimum distributions at age $70^1/_2$. Alternately, he can convert to payout annuities that provide:

• fixed, equity indexed, or variable payments;

• payments that increase at a fixed rate, say two or three percent each year;

• payments that change gradually with a cost-of-living index;

• a lump-sum cash-out option; and

• a joint and survivor benefit (usually an annuity over the joint lifetimes of IRA jowner and spouse) that is increased if the co-annuitant dies or there is a divorce.

This is merely the beginning. Ask a financial advisor to investigate what's currently available in IRA annuities. If you can't get imaginative features like these, ask for them anyway. The insurer may just add a rider to your present policy that brings it up-to-date.

13.

You inherit an IRA

"They (the heirs) make money the old-fashioned way. They inherit it."
Brian Morgan

IRAs aren't only about account owners taking minimum distributions and passing what's left to beneficiaries. It's quite possible you'll be the one who inherits a significant account from parents or a rich uncle. In this chapter, let's consider how to look at an IRA when you are its designated beneficiary.

Example: You are Carol, age 45, the daughter of John Martin. He dies in 2003, naming you the beneficiary of his $1 million traditional IRA. To make matters interesting, let's say John left behind an additional $2.5 million, for total assets of $3.5 million. The estate taxes are $750,000. Here are some of the issues to consider:

• Since you aren't John's surviving spouse, it's not possible to rollover his IRA to your personal account. In other words, you can't defer taking withdrawals and let the account build up until you reach age 70½. Nor can you stretch out distributions slowly using fictional life expectancies in the IRS Uniform Lifetime

Table. (See Chapter 6.) Instead, you must begin taking at least minimum amounts from the account in 2004 based on your fixed life expectancy at age 46.

Some good news: The first year's required minimum distribution will be only 2.6385 percent of the account's value on December 31, 2003. This percentage is determined by dividing one by .379, using your 37.9 year IRS life expectancy at age 46.[22] Of course the divisor changes (to .369, .359, .349, etc.) in the following years. Certainly, you'd be wise to take merely the minimum taxable amount from your father's IRA and let the remainder grow without taxes. If necessary, you'll spend all personal non-IRA income and liquidate or amortize other assets fully. The account will always be there if you need it.

• As you study the situation, you notice that your son, Tommy (age seven) is contingent beneficiary of the IRA and would have inherited the account if you had predeceased John. If Tommy were the beneficiary, you recognize that his minimum distributions would be much smaller - actually, his divisor would be only .748 at age eight (Exhibit A), and his first distribution percentage would be merely 1.3369 percent (1÷.748). Compare this with your percentages mentioned in the previous paragraph.

What you can do: If you disclaim (refuse) the IRA, the law substitutes Tommy as designated beneficiary

22 See the IRS unisex life expectancy table (Exhibit A) at the end of this chapter.

of the account. This won't be a taxable gift to anyone either.

A word of caution: Obviously, you should be well fixed financially to consider disclaiming your father's IRA. But, if you do disclaim, Tommy will have an optimum tax deferral plan and an excellent start on his education, retirement, and future financial security. This might even enable you to spend other personal funds freely on yourself or leave more to charity. Get good legal counsel as you review all the possibilities. Once made, a decision to disclaim is not reversible.

• If there are estate obligations, and there isn't enough cash in John's estate, his personal representative may want you to take from the IRA to pay bills. A personal bank loan that helps preserve the account would be better. Now is the time to consider this if you must come up with some money to help with debts and estate taxes.

To summarize, if you inherit an IRA, review the suitability of a minimum distributions plan, the possibility of a disclaimer, and the likelihood you'll need to borrow to pay estate obligations. In the next chapter, we'll look at how the payment of estate taxes actually reduces income taxes on your IRA distributions.

Exhibit A

(IRS unisex single life expectancies - ages 1-55)

Age of IRA Owner Or Designated Beneficiary	Expectancy (Years)	Age of IRA Owner Or Designated Beneficiary	Expectancy (Years)
0	82.4	28	55.3
1	81.6	29	54.3
2	80.6	30	53.3
3	79.7	31	52.4
4	78.7	32	51.4
5	77.7	33	50.4
6	76.7	34	49.4
7	75.8	35	48.5
8	74.8	36	47.5
9	73.8	37	46.5
10	72.8	38	45.6
11	71.8	39	44.6
12	70.8	40	43.6
13	69.9	41	42.7
14	68.9	42	41.7
15	67.9	43	40.7
16	66.9	44	39.8
17	66.0	45	38.8
18	65.0	46	37.9
19	64.0	47	37.0
20	63.0	48	36.0
21	62.1	49	35.1
22	61.1	50	34.2
23	60.1	51	33.3
24	59.1	52	32.3
25	58.2	53	31.4
26	57.2	54	30.5
27	56.2	55	29.6

14.

Paying estate taxes on an inherited IRA

"I'd love to go to Washington - if only to be near my money." Bob Hope

In chapter 13, I assume you inherited your father's $1 million IRA which was merely one asset in his $2.5 million estate. And, his estate's representative paid a $750,000 estate tax to transfer everything to the heirs. Let's look at how this tax payment affects you once matters are cleared up and the estate is closed:

First, you'll need to determine the IRA's portion of these estate taxes. Actually, if your father hadn't owned the $1 million IRA, his estate would have been worth merely $1.5 million ($2.5 million less $1 million), and let's say the estate tax would have been only $250,000. In other words, the $1 million IRA's slice of these taxes was $500,000 ($750,000 less $250,000). Know also that some of this estate tax is paid over to your father's state of residence. Assume the ratio is 95-5 (federal and state), so $475,000 is the federal portion, and $25,000 is the state's share.

The bottom line: If you cash-out the IRA, you'll claim a federal income tax deduction of $475,000 - the federal government's share of the IRA's $500,000

in estate taxes. Here's how this deduction impacts the income tax you'll pay:

$1,000,000	taxable IRA income
-475,000	deduction for federal estate taxes
$525,000	taxable income (federal)
-183,750	federal income taxes (assume 35% of $525,000)
$816,250	Net IRA after income taxes ($1 million less $183,750)
$316,250	Net IRA after estate and income taxes [$1 million less $683,750 ($500,000, plus $183,750)]

[In other words, even though your income tax rate is 35 percent, you'll only pay taxes of about $183,750 (18 percent), and you'll net over $800,000 after income taxes are paid.]

Alternately, if you liquidate the $1 million IRA slowly, taking required minimum distributions, you'll likely claim income tax deductions *dollar for dollar* until the $475,000 amount is completely used up. (In effect, the first $475,000 in IRA distributions should be completely tax-free. Thereafter, all withdrawals will be fully taxable.)

Some more possible good news: Let's say your father left his $1.5 million in non-IRA assets to George, your brother, and the will charged all estate taxes to George's inheritance. In our example, you'll still be entitled to deduct $475,000 against your IRA as it is cashed-out or distributed over time. *My suggestion:* Keep in contact with your father's lawyer and estate representative even if you receive nothing under the will. You will want to know whether the IRA bears any obligation for estate taxes; even if it doesn't, you'll still need the tax information to deduct estate taxes against your taxable IRA distributions.

In summary, an IRA beneficiary will always pay income taxes on distributions from a traditional IRA. The deceased's personal estate representative may also pay on estate tax levied on the transfer of this account. But, since the federal portion of this estate tax qualifies as an income tax deduction, all IRA beneficiaries must pay attention to gain a valuable tax break in the law.

15.

Using life insurance to protect an IRA's value

"I don't want to tell you how much insurance I have with Prudential - All I can say is: When I go, they go!" Jack Benny

In chapters 13 and 14, I assumed you were the daughter-beneficiary of John Martin's $1 million traditional IRA. His personal representative paid a $500,000 estate tax to transfer the account, and you paid $183,750 in income taxes just to inherit this money. Consequently, you could say the IRA's after-tax value is only $316,250 or about 30 cents on the dollar. That isn't much for all of John's time and work to become an IRA millionaire.

Let's step back and assume that 10 years ago - when the IRA was worth only $400,000 - your father had a conference with his lawyer, accountant and financial planner. Some projections indicated the possibility of (a) a $1 million account someday, and (b) a taxable estate of nearly $3 million as well. Fortunately, John decided to pay $10,000 in annual premiums for a $500,000 life insurance policy to help cover the taxes that would be due. He also created a trust that owned this policy when he died.

Initially, John was reluctant to gift the $10,000 premiums just to protect his estate for others, thinking he might need this money eventually. His advisors understood, but persisted gently. As everything became clear, John agreed to the coverage, and he reached the following conclusions:

• Since the insurance trust would be written carefully, he could claim a gift tax exclusion for the premium-gifts. There wouldn't be any gift tax to pay.

• If he couldn't afford the $10,000 gifts from non-IRA assets, he could withdraw some money from his IRA for premiums. Since there would be an income tax of say, 33 percent, he was prepared to take out up to $15,000 to cover both premium and the tax payment.

• If (a) the $400,000 IRA earned eight percent annually on average, and (b) even he withdrew as much as $40,000 annually for gifts, taxes and living expenses, the money would last for nearly another 20 years.

• Should his IRA be completely liquidated by death, the insurance ($500,000) would more than replace (a) the gross value ($400,000) of his present account, and (b) the net value ($316,250) of his projected $1 million IRA balance.

• Finally, if he died prematurely his children might have both IRA and the insurance proceeds. And, if they were lucky enough to avoid paying any estate taxes, the income tax-free insurance would still be available for emergencies. This would also help assure a stretch-like minimum distributions plan for the IRA.

My suggestions: If you have a significant IRA, life insurance enhances the overall financial plan. Choose a quality policy from a sound insurer, (b) structure the policyowner and beneficiary correctly, and (c) work out premium payment approaches that make this affordable.

16.

Keeping tax and transfer problems to a minimum

"Money is like mulch, not good unless spread." Francis Bacon

Congress certainly gives IRA owners plenty of ups and downs. On the positive side, there are tax deductions, tax deferral until age $70^1/_2$, and even tax postponement thereafter and for generations-to-come. On the minus side, you might lose control to poor beneficiary arrangements or estate taxes that cause premature liquidation of the account. IRAs aren't good assets for a spouse's trust either, since the account may be fully distributed over his or her actual life expectancy. Finally, even if everything passes smoothly to descendants, it's still possible an IRA will be lost to mismanagement or unexpected circumstances.

Here's a simple strategy that minimizes all these issues: Enjoy the IRA for as long as you (and spouse, if any) live; then, donate what's left to a favorite charity.

Example: Let's say you are age $70^1/_2$ and have a $500,000 IRA. Your plan is to take minimum distributions and name children beneficiaries of what remains at death. You are aware of the "8 percent" example in Chapter 6 where the account is worth $800,000 at your age 89. But, you don't like the complications IRA's present for the family.

Instead, you name a charity to become the ultimate beneficiary of what remains in the account. In the meantime, you might take a little extra from the IRA for premiums and establish an insurance trust to own a policy for family. *The bottom line:* You convert a potential problem (the taxable IRA) into a solution (a charitable gift and a protected insurance trust.) What's the appropriate amount of insurance? That's up to you, but something like $300,000 or $400,000 might do fine.

If you like this idea, here are a few additional charitable tax planning concepts:

• If you wonder about whether IRAs can own life insurance, that's not permitted in the law. Consequently, your policy should be held in the trust instead.

• You can gift cash from your account to charity while alive and claim a tax deduction of up to 50 percent of adjusted gross income. You'll also include the donation in taxable income that year under current (2002) law. When an IRA passes to charity at death, however, neither the institution nor your estate pays income taxes on the transfer.

• Assume your will already leaves, say, a $100,000 cash bequest to charity. You also have a $100,000 traditional IRA payable to children that's worth much less after taxes. Reverse these transactions. Give the IRA to charity and leave cash to your children - the charity gets the same and your children get more.

• It's possible to leave an IRA to a trust that pays income to a child while alive; then, at her death a charity receives what's left. In the meantime, there won't be required minimum distributions, either. This intriguing concept is getting attention in the press.

In summary, if you believe a traditional IRA is a complex asset in an estate plan, you are correct! There is a simpler approach. Leave the account to charity, and purchase an insurance policy for family to "replace" the account.

17.

IRAs in large estates

"Wealth and power are much more likely to be the result of breeding than they are of reading." Fran Lebowitz

In estates of $1 million or more, IRAs present some special challenges for your advisors. Let me explain:

Assume a $1 million IRA payable to your spouse, Mary. You own another $2 million consisting of a home and some miscellaneous investments. These are mostly in joint name with Mary or left to her under your will.

The objective: Pass everything to family in a tax-effective manner. Your lawyer prepares the following "menu" for you to consider:

(A) Keep everything as is. If you predecease Mary, there will be no estate taxes at your death since all property passing to a spouse is estate tax-free. *The problem:* When Mary dies, only $1 million (2003) is tax-exempt, and your heirs will pay transfer taxes on $2 million to inherit the property.

(B) Leave $2 million to Mary and $1 million to a "family trust" for Mary and children. Since the trust is not part of her taxable estate, your heirs will pay transfer taxes on only $1 million ($2 million, less her $1 million exemption), assuming she survives you. But, if she predeceases, they'll still pay taxes on $2 million.

(C) Split the $3 million equally. Then, both Mary and you create family trusts to receive $1 million at death. *The result:* This assures each estate a $1 million exemption; consequently, your family always pays transfer taxes on only $1 million - a possible winning alternative.

The real issue with (C) is what to do with the $1 million IRA. When you divide assets equally with Mary, your $1.5 million share will consist of (a) a $1 million IRA, and (b) $500,000 in other assets; she'll own $1.5 million in non-IRA property. Since you'll leave $1 million to the family trust, it's likely this will be the $1 million IRA. *The problem:* IRAs aren't good assets for trusts. A trustee can't rollover the account, and it probably must take withdrawals over Mary's actual IRS life expectancy. *The result:* Your IRA will be liquidated more rapidly (causing higher income taxes) than if Mary was its direct beneficiary.

To summarize, in larger estates an optimal estate plan will probably consist of (a) dividing assets between spouses, and (b) each mate leaving the $1 million "exemption" (2003) to a family trust for the survivor. Unfortunately, this arrangement is more complicated when a significant IRA ends up payable to the trust. In effect, a choice must be made between estate tax savings and income tax deferral - all this and more in uncertain planning times where the results always depend on exactly when you die.[23] *My suggestions:* Be well informed; do the best you can; and, review your circumstances regularly with knowledgeable advisors.

---

23 Under present law, the estate tax exemption increases after 2003 until 2010 (from $1 million gradually to $3.5 million). In 2010, the exemption is 100 percent of your estate; thereafter, it is only $1 million.

Notes: